2/10

California

Rich Smith

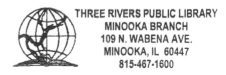

Visit us at
www.abdopublishing.com

Published by ABDO Publishing Company, 8000 West 78th Street, Suite 310, Edina, Minnesota 55439 USA. Copyright ©2010 by Abdo Consulting Group, Inc. International copyrights reserved in all countries. No part of this book may be reproduced in any form without written permission from the publisher. The Checkerboard Library™ is a trademark and logo of ABDO Publishing Company.

Printed in the United States.

Editor: John Hamilton
Graphic Design: Sue Hamilton
Cover Illustration: Neil Klinepier
Cover Photo: iStock Photo
Interior Photo Credits: Alamy, AP Images, Bancroft Library-University of California Berkeley, Comstock, Corbis, Getty, Granger Collection, iStock Photo, Jerry Ting, Library of Congress, Mile High Maps, Mountain High Maps, One Mile Up, Photo Researchers Inc, U.S. Navy, and U.S. Postal Service.
Statistics: State population statistics taken from 2008 U.S. Census Bureau estimates. City and town population statistics taken from July 1, 2007, U.S. Census Bureau estimates. Land and water area statistics taken from 2000 Census, U.S. Census Bureau.

Manufactured with paper containing at least 10% post-consumer waste

Library of Congress Cataloging-in-Publication Data

Smith, Rich, 1954-
  California / Rich Smith.
      p. cm.
  Includes index.
  ISBN 978-1-60453-640-9
  1. California--Juvenile literature. I. Title.

F861.3.S65 2010
979.4--dc22

2008051010

Table of Contents

The Golden State

In California, dreams often come true. That is why millions of people from every corner of the world have made California their home. California is called the Golden State. But an even better nickname might be the Dream State.

Most of California has pleasant weather. Not too warm in summer, not too cold in winter. There are many natural wonders, including snow-covered mountains and fearsome deserts. California has beautiful beaches and bays, and forests thick with tall trees.

Many important businesses are in California. They are helped by the state's excellent roads, railways, harbors, and airports. California attracts people with important skills and the ability to dream big dreams.

The Golden Gate Bridge is 1.7 miles (2.7 km) long and connects San Francisco with Marin County.

Quick Facts

CALIFORNIA REPUBLIC

Name: The word California comes from the name of Queen Califia, a character in a Spanish novel written in 1510. Queen Califia ruled over a paradise rich in gold.

State Capital: Sacramento, population 460,242

Date of Statehood: September 9, 1850 (31st state)

Population: 36,756,666 (the most populous state)

Area (Total Land and Water): 163,696 square miles (423,971 sq km), 3rd-largest state

Largest City: Los Angeles, population 3,834,340

Nickname: The Golden State

Motto: *Eureka* ("I have found it!")

State Animal: Grizzly Bear

State Bird: Valley Quail

Poppy

Serpentine

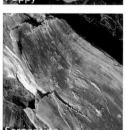
Redwood Trees

Richard Nixon

State Flower: Poppy

State Rock: Serpentine

State Tree: Redwood

State Song: "I Love You, California"

Highest Point: Mount Whitney, 14,505 feet (4,421 m)

Lowest Point: Death Valley, 282 feet (86 m) below sea level (lowest point in all of North America)

Average July Temperature: 73°F (23°C)

Record High Temperature: 134°F (57°C), July 10, 1913

Average January Temperature: 50°F (10°C)

Record Low Temperature: -45°F (-43°C), January 20, 1937

Average Annual Precipitation: 23 inches (58 cm)

Number of U.S. Senators: 2

Number of U.S. Representatives: 53

U.S. Presidents Born in California: Richard Nixon (1913-1994), 37th president

U.S. Postal Service Abbreviation: CA

Geography

California is on the West Coast of the United States. The state is 800 miles (1,287 km) long from north to south. It is 375 miles (604 km) wide from east to west at its widest point.

California has a long, beach-filled coastline bordering the Pacific Ocean. Large bays make safe harbors for ships. Inland, there are fertile valleys, mountain ranges, glaciers, volcanoes, forests, lakes, and deserts.

The Central Valley is a large plain that has excellent soil for growing crops. It is approximately 450 miles (724 km) long and 50 miles (80 km) wide. The Sacramento and San Joaquin Rivers run through the Central Valley.

California's total land and water area is 163,696 square miles (423,971 sq km). It is the third-largest state.
The state capital is Sacramento.

West of the Central Valley is a chain of rolling hills and low mountains. This is the Coast Range.

To the east of the Central Valley is a 400-mile-long (644 km) wall of mighty granite peaks called the Sierra

Mount Whitney is the highest point in California.

Nevada. This mountain range is home to Mount Whitney. It is 14,505 feet (4,421 m) tall, the highest point in the state.

Northern California contains the Klamath Mountains and the Cascade Range. This thickly forested area has many steep, rugged canyons. The Cascade Range contains a chain of volcanoes. They include Mount Shasta and Lassen Peak.

Southern California includes the Channel Islands. They are a 160-mile-long (257 km) chain of islands in the Pacific Ocean. Santa Catalina Island is the only one with a large number of people living on it. Five of the other islands form a national park.

Southeastern California contains the Colorado and Mojave Deserts. Death Valley is one of the driest and hottest places on Earth. It is the lowest point in North America, at 282 feet (86 m) below sea level.

Death Valley averages less than 2 inches (5 cm) of rain per year.

Climate and Weather

California's coastal regions have mild summers and winters.

California's large size means it has several different climate zones.

The coastal regions have mild summers and winters. The Central Valley has hot summers and cool winters. The mountain regions have cool summers and arctic-like winters. The deserts have hot summers and cool winters.

The rainfall average for the entire state is about 23 inches (58 cm) per year.

Most of the rain falls between October and April. Winter snow is common far inland on the higher mountains. The rainiest part of California is the northwest region.

The cold ocean currents flowing along the California coast come from the far north. That causes the state's central and northern shoreline to often be blanketed in thick fog.

Thick fog covers the Golden Gate Bridge.

Plants and Animals

Forests cover more than one-third of all the land in California. On the western slopes of the Sierra Nevada grow giant sequoia trees. They can reach the height of a 20-story building, more than 250 feet (76 m) tall. An even taller cousin of the giant sequoia is the coast redwood. The biggest coast redwoods have tops 375 feet (114 m) in the air.

No other tree on Earth grows as tall as a coast redwood.

The oldest tree found anywhere is the Great Basin bristlecone pine. It lives for several thousands of years.

Joshua trees are found mainly in the Mojave Desert. They have round clusters of 12-inch (30-cm) spikes instead of leaves at the ends of their branches.

Mormon pioneers named these trees "Joshua" because the trees looked like the prophet Joshua holding his arms up and waving the settlers on to the Promised Land.

Many kinds of grasses and wildflowers are found throughout California. The most familiar is the poppy. It is the official flower of California.

The valley quail is the state's official bird. It is gray and plump and has a thin plume of black feathers on top of its head. The valley quail likes walking and running better than flying.

The California condor, once a common sight, is now on the endangered list. The California grizzly bear is extinct. However, California is still home to a great variety of animals including sea lions, seals, jackrabbits, deer, bobcats, black bears, coyotes, and pumas.

The northern part of California has rivers where salmon spawn. Salmon are a favorite fish of Californians. However, the official state sea creature is the gray whale. It passes by the California coast on its annual migration to and from the warm winter waters of Mexico.

California's official state sea creature is the gray whale.

California Condor

Elephant Seal

Ground Squirrel

History

California was first settled by people from Asia. This happened thousands of years before the first European explorers arrived.

The first European to visit California was Juan Rodriguez Cabrillo. He claimed the area for Spain in 1542. In 1769, Captain Gaspar de Portola arrived at today's San Diego. He and his soldiers built a fort there. They built another fort 400 miles (644 km) north at Monterey.

Explorer of California 1542
29 USA
Juan Rodríguez CABRILLO

Franciscan monks built missions in California. These were places of beautiful Spanish architecture where they taught Native Americans about Christianity.

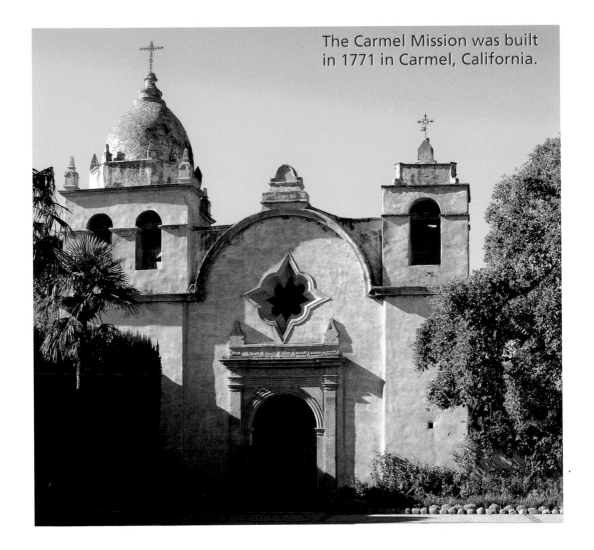

The Carmel Mission was built in 1771 in Carmel, California.

The first Spanish colonists arrived in 1776. They made their homes in San Francisco. Other Spanish settlers started towns in places up and down the state. They also colonized Mexico. In 1821, the Mexican colonists won independence from Spain. They also won control over California.

In the 1840s, pioneers from the young United States pushed west to the Pacific Ocean. Fighting broke out between the Mexican citizens of

The Mexican-American War was fought from 1846 until 1848.

California and the settlers from the United States. The angry Mexican government told the United States to get its Navy and Army out of California. The United States refused, which led to war. The Mexican-American War lasted from 1846 until 1848.

After winning the war, the United States gained control of California.

James W. Marshall discovered the first pieces of gold at Sutter's Mill in January 1848.

Less than two weeks after the war ended, gold was discovered in California. It was found at a place called Sutter's Mill on the American River near Sacramento. James Wilson Marshall discovered the first pieces of gold in January 1848.

People from all over the world rushed to California. Dreams of striking it rich filled their heads. Thousands of people came by land and sea. The first big group of gold-seekers reached California in 1849. They became known as the Forty-Niners.

Governor Peter Burnett

California became an official state on September 9, 1850. Peter Hardeman Burnett was California's first governor.

Gold fever cooled off by the early 1850s. But that did not stop people from moving to California. The Golden State was seen by many as a land of wonder and opportunity.

Industries took hold in California in the early 1900s. In 1907, the first movie was made in California. This gave birth to Hollywood as the movie capital of the world. Military airplanes were built in California beginning in 1912. Today the state is an important center of the aerospace industry.

California's population grew after World War II. Many soldiers, sailors, and aviators spent time in California. Some fell in love with the state. They saw California as a great place to live, buy a home, and raise a family.

Producer and director D.W. Griffith was one of America's first and most successful Hollywood filmmakers.

Did You Know?

- A huge flock of swallows returns every year to the old Spanish mission at San Juan Capistrano. The little birds arrive at the mission without fail every March 19. This has been happening since the early 1800s, not long after the mission was built. The swallows stay there until October 23. No one can explain why the swallows always come and go on those exact two days.

- Earthquakes are common in California. One of the worst happened in 1906 in San Francisco. The powerful earthquake struck on the morning of April 18. Many buildings completely collapsed during the shaking. The earthquake also broke most of the city's water pipes. Firefighters had no water to put out the flames that erupted inside the collapsed buildings. Fire raged for three days in the heart of the city. Approximately 3,000 people were killed in the disaster.

People

Actor **Leonardo DiCaprio** (1974–) was born in Los Angeles. After working briefly in TV, he began working in movies. He became a superstar after starring in the 1997 blockbuster *Titanic*. DiCaprio is an environmentalist who uses his star power to educate people about conserving energy.

George Lucas Steven Spielberg

Filmmaker **George Lucas** (1944–) was born in Modesto. He is a famous director, producer, and screenwriter. In 1977 he created the blockbuster movie *Star Wars.* Lucas also worked on the Indiana Jones movies, along with his friend and fellow Californian Steven Spielberg.

Ronald Reagan (1911–2004) was the 40th president of the United States. He served from 1981 until 1989. He was born in Illinois, but moved to Los Angeles in the 1930s. He was a famous actor for many years. He served as governor of California from 1967 until 1975. Reagan was a Republican who wanted to limit government and cut taxes.

Michelle Kwan (1980–) is one of the greatest figure skaters in the world. She was born in Torrance, California. She has won many U.S. and world championships. She has won two Olympic medals. Her figure skating style is very graceful and artistic.

In 1983, **Sally Ride** (1951–) became the first American woman astronaut to go into outer space. She was born and raised in Los Angeles. She joined the space program in 1978. On June 18, 1983, she rode the space shuttle *Challenger* into orbit around the earth. She also flew into space in 1984. Today she works as a teacher and author.

César Chavez (1927–1993) was a civil rights leader who tried to improve the lives of farm workers. He fought for higher wages and better working conditions. He worked as a farm laborer in California before becoming active in politics. In 1962, he started a labor union that became known as the United Farm Workers of America.

Tiger Woods (1975–) is one of the most successful golfers ever to play the game. He has been ranked number one in the world many times. He was born in 1975 in Cypress, California, a suburb of Los Angeles. He started playing golf as a young child. Today he is a very popular sports figure. His skill has inspired many people to play golf.

Steve Jobs (1955–) is the founder and chairman of Apple, Inc., maker of Apple computers, iPods, and other electronic devices. He was born in 1955 in San Francisco. In the late 1970s and early 1980s, he helped make personal computers popular. Jobs believes computers should be easy to use, stylish, and functional.

Cities

Sacramento is California's state capital. It has a population of 460,242. It is the seventh-largest city in California. Sacramento is located in the northern part of the Central Valley. It is about 75 miles (121 km) inland from San Francisco Bay. Giant ocean-going cargo ships can reach Sacramento by sailing up the deep and wide Sacramento River.

Los Angeles is California's largest city. It is the second-biggest city in the nation. About 3,834,340 people call it home. Cities in the surrounding area hold many millions more. Los Angeles sprawls over more than 469 square miles (1,215 sq km). The city is famous for its freeways, movie studios, and palm trees. It is also well known for its aerospace industries, technology companies, and international trade activities. It has an airport and seaport that are among the busiest in the world.

San Diego, with 1,266,731 residents, is the second-largest city in California. It is about 100 miles (161 km) south of Los Angeles. Mexico is only a few miles away. San Diego has one of the country's biggest Navy bases. Nearby is one of the biggest Marine Corps camps. The city has a very pleasant climate, beautiful beaches, great hotels, and many famous attractions. Tourism is an important industry for San Diego. Other industries include biotechnology research and electronics.

San Francisco is the oldest California city. It is the home of the Golden Gate Bridge

and cable cars. Famous for fog, San Francisco is located at the entrance to San Francisco Bay. Because of chilling fog in the mornings and evenings, summer temperatures are sometimes colder than those in winter. San Francisco is the state's financial center. Among its attractions are a colorful waterfront and many historic neighborhoods. San Francisco's population of 764,976 makes it the 14th-largest city in the United States.

Transportation

California's 17,300-mile (27,842 km) highway system is among the best in the nation. A typical California highway carries as many as 51,000 cars, trucks, and buses every day.

Thousands of vehicles travel over California's highways every day.

Cargo ships use 12 major seaports in California, including those in Los Angeles, Long Beach, and Oakland.

About 25 freight-train companies operate on tracks statewide. Amtrak carries passengers in and out of California aboard comfortable trains on seven different routes.

There are 31 commercial airports in California. The two busiest are the Los Angeles International Airport and San Francisco International Airport. Los Angeles International Airport ranks fifth in the world for passenger volume. The state also has about 230 other public airports. It has more than 20 military airfields.

A plane takes off from Los Angeles International Airport.

Natural Resources

California raises twice as much food as any other state. Grapes, tomatoes, oranges, lemons, nuts, asparagus, apricots, figs, milk products, poultry, and beef all come from California. The state's agriculture industry earns approximately $32 billion per year.

Salmon, crab, sablefish, squid, and jack mackerel are among the main catches of California's commercial fishermen. The roughly $110-million bounty caught in their nets each year makes California the nation's sixth-biggest supplier of fish.

A big catch!

Forestry is another big business in California. Each year, the state's forests provide

The Pacific Lumber Company in Scotia, CA, is one of the largest redwood lumber mills in the world.

billions of feet of fir, pine, cedar, and redwood lumber.

More than 20 different types of minerals are mined or quarried in California. These include Portland cement, construction sand and gravel, boron, soda ash, pumice, pyrophyllite, magnesium, feldspar, serpentine, and perlite. Gold is also mined in California. Benitoite, sometimes called "the blue diamond," is the state gemstone.

Fossil fuels are another important California resource. Ten percent of the nation's crude oil and natural gas needs are met by California.

Industry

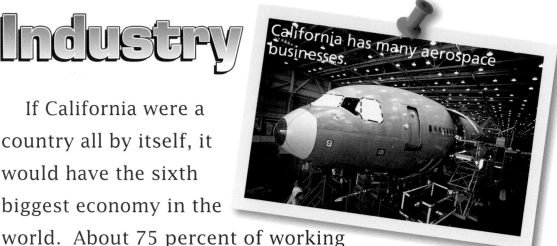

California has many aerospace businesses.

If California were a country all by itself, it would have the sixth biggest economy in the world. About 75 percent of working Californians have jobs in either the Los Angeles or San Francisco Bay areas. These two areas process food, produce clothing, and make electronics, computers, software, aerospace technology, and machinery. The Los Angeles and San Francisco regions also are the headquarters of leading banks, investment brokerages, consulting groups, insurance agencies, real estate developers, construction contractors, and many other service companies.

Another important part of the California economy is the entertainment industry. Movies, music, television shows, video games, books, magazines, and other forms of entertainment are produced in California.

Tourism is also important. Many people vacation in California. In a typical year, tourists spend at least $75 billion while visiting.

Visitors enjoy California's Disneyland.

Sports

California has 27 professional sports teams, more than any other state. California has hosted the Olympic Games three times. The first was in 1932 at Los Angeles for the Summer Olympics. The second was in 1960 at Squaw Valley for the Winter Olympics. The third was in 1984 in Los Angeles for the Summer Olympics.

California's universities have some of the best amateur sports teams in the world. The oldest and best-known college contest in California is the Rose

Bowl football game, which is traditionally held on New Year's Day.

More than 90,000 fans attend the Rose Bowl football game.

Popular outdoor recreation includes surfing, sailing, skateboarding, and fishing. Also big are snow skiing and snowboarding. Bicycling, jogging, hiking, camping, and hunting are enjoyed as well.

The best-known park in California is breathtaking Yosemite National Park. The state has many other national parks, monuments, and protected wilderness areas.

Yosemite National Park is California's most well-known wilderness area.

Entertainment

La Brea Tar Pits

Alcatraz

Culture is a source of great pride among Californians. The state has many museums, theaters, concert halls, zoos, aquariums, and amusement parks.

Los Angeles has the West's largest natural history museum. A few miles away are the La Brea Tar Pits, where trapped prehistoric animals died long ago.

The San Francisco Bay island prison of Alcatraz once held America's kings of crime, but now is a popular museum.

Major zoos are located in Los Angeles, San Diego, San Francisco, and San Jose. San Diego is also home to Sea World, which is part marine aquarium and part amusement park.

Disneyland, in the city of Anaheim, is California's most familiar amusement park. Others include Six Flags Magic Mountain, Knott's Berry Farm, and Universal Studios Hollywood.

Californians love parades. That is why each New Year's Day more than one million citizens line the streets of Pasadena to watch the Tournament of Roses

Parade. This popular event is famous for its floats. Every float in the Rose Parade is covered top to bottom with flower petals.

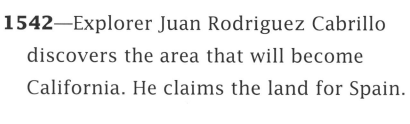

Timeline

10,000 BC—First settlers from Asia arrive.

1542—Explorer Juan Rodriguez Cabrillo discovers the area that will become California. He claims the land for Spain.

1769—Captain Gaspar de Portola builds Spain's first forts in California. Franciscan monks begin building missions.

1776—First settlers from Spain arrive.

1821—Spanish rule of California ends. Mexican rule begins.

1840—First settlers from the United States arrive in California.

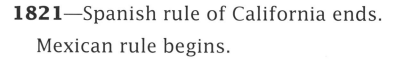

1848—Mexico loses California after the Mexican-American War.

1849—Gold causes people worldwide to rush into California.

1850—California becomes the 31st state.

1869—Transcontinental railroad completed. Connects California to rest of the country.

1907—First filming of a movie in Los Angeles. The Hollywood film industry is born.

1912—First military aircraft is built. California's aerospace industry is born.

1946—Returning World War II soldiers help make California the most populated state.

2003—Former actor Arnold Schwarzenegger is elected governor of California.

Glossary

Aerospace—A branch of industry and technology that is involved with both aviation and space flight.

Biotechnology—Using biological processes for industry. Growing small microorganisms to make medicines is an example of biotechnology.

Climate—Weather conditions that normally occur in an area over a long period of time.

Crude Oil—Oil that comes straight out of the ground, before it has been processed, or refined, into such products as gasoline or heating oil.

Environmentalist—A person who is concerned about the natural world, and who wants to protect and preserve it.

Mexican-American War—In the 1840s, fighting broke out between the Mexican citizens in the southwest and the settlers from the United States. The angry Mexican government told the United States to get its Navy and Army out of California. The United States refused, which led to war. The Mexican-American War lasted from 1846 until 1848.

Migration—When large numbers of animals move from one region to another, usually because of a change in the seasons.

Mission—A large building or fort that Christians used as a base to spread their religion to the local people. Spanish missions in California were also used to govern the new colony.

Plain—A large area of flat land, with very few trees.

Spawn—When fish, frogs, crustaceans, or other water creatures, lay their eggs.

World War II—A conflict across the world, lasting from 1939-1945. The U.S. entered the war in December 1941.

Index